NIGHTMARE ISLAND

More Spine-Chilling Books from Harper Trophy

HALLOWEEN: STORIES AND POEMS
edited by Caroline Feller Bauer

DEVIL'S DONKEY
by Bill Brittain

DR. DREDD'S WAGON OF WONDERS
by Bill Brittain

WHO KNEW THERE'D BE GHOSTS?
by Bill Brittain

THE WISH GIVER: THREE TALES OF COVEN TREE
by Bill Brittain

THE PIT
by Ann Cheetham

T.J.'S GHOST
by Shirley Climo

DRACULA IS A PAIN IN THE NECK
by Elizabeth Levy

FRANKENSTEIN MOVED IN ON THE FOURTH FLOOR
by Elizabeth Levy

NIGHTWAVES: SCARY TALES FOR AFTER DARK
by Collin McDonald

SCARY STORIES TO TELL IN THE DARK
by Alvin Schwartz

MORE SCARY STORIES TO TELL IN THE DARK
by Alvin Schwartz

**SCARY STORIES 3: MORE TALES
TO CHILL YOUR BONES**
by Alvin Schwartz

NIGHTMARE ISLAND

And Other Real-Life Mysteries

JIM RAZZI

ILLUSTRATED BY
JOHN JUDE PALENCAR

HarperTrophy
A Division of HarperCollins Publishers

Nightmare Island
And Other Real-Life Mysteries
Text copyright © 1993 by Jim Razzi
Illustrations copyright © 1993 by John Jude Palencar
Typography by Stefanie Rosenfeld
3   4   5   6   7   8   9   10
❖
First Harper Trophy edition

Library of Congress Cataloging-in-Publication Data
Razzi, Jim.
    Nightmare island, and other real-life mysteries /
Jim Razzi ; illustrated by John Jude Palencar.
        p.   cm.
    Summary: Describes an assortment of unusual
events, including a weeping statue, a ghostly summons,
and a teenager who saw her own future.
    ISBN 0-06-440426-9 (pbk.)
    1. Curiosities and wonders—Juvenile literature.
[1. Curiosities and wonders.   2. Parapsychology.]
I. Palencar, John Jude, ill.   II. Title.
AG243.R33   1993   92-32638
031.02—dc20   CIP
                                           AC

CONTENTS

It sounds impossible, but everything in this book really happened. The events you will read about here defy explanation. You cannot come up with logical reasons for why they occurred. You may not even believe they are true. But they have all been reported by reliable witnesses. In many cases, they have factual evidence to back them up.

Believe it or not, strange things don't happen only in the imagination. Real life is full of mysteries that no one has been able to solve. But see for yourself. . . .

NIGHTMARE ISLAND
A Deadly Dream Come True

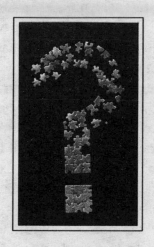

Can a nightmare come true? You
might not think so. But if Byron
Somes were still alive, he would have
to disagree with you.

On August 27, 1883, Byron Somes, a reporter for *The Boston Globe*, stayed late at the office to catch up on some work. His chores accomplished, Byron rubbed his forehead and sighed. It had been a long night. He propped his head on his arms on the desk and closed his eyes. Soon he was fast asleep.

A short time later, Byron woke up with a start, trembling from head to foot. He had just had a terrible nightmare. He looked at the office clock. It was 3:00 A.M. Byron gazed around the empty office, trying to clear his head. He couldn't stop shaking. His dream had been so dreadful.

He had seen scores of people on a far-off island, running in terror as they tried to escape a sea of hot molten lava. A giant volcano had just erupted. The explosion had been tremendous. He had seen the island disintegrating and sinking into the sea before his eyes.

His nightmare had been so vivid that he couldn't stop thinking about it. At last, with a trembling hand, Byron reached for a pencil and paper. Perhaps writing about it would help calm his nerves.

The nightmare had seemed so real that Byron was able to report it as if it had really happened. No detail had escaped him: it was as if he had been watching the catastrophe from some vantage point in the sky. Even the name of the island came to him. It was called *Pralape*.

Byron wrote and wrote. He described the terrifying explosion of the erupting volcano that had ripped the island

apart. He told of the thousands of people who had fled from the sliding mud and fast-moving lava, only to die in the boiling sea.

At last Byron laid down his pen. He felt exhausted. He left the report on his desk and made his way home.

Later that morning, his editor found the story on Byron's desk. The story surprised the editor, who hadn't heard of the disaster. Believing that somehow Byron must have gotten a scoop, he splashed the report across the front page of *The Boston Globe* in banner headlines. The story was quickly wired all across America. Readers waited breathlessly for more information on the catastrophe—the mightiest volcanic explosion that had ever been recorded!

Byron stayed home that day and did not hear the news until his editor contacted him and asked for more details of the disaster. Immediately, Byron realized that a mistake had been made. He quickly told his editor the truth—the entire event had just been a nightmare.

The editor was flabbergasted. *The Globe* was going to be the laughingstock of the country.

The editor tried to withdraw the story before any more damage could be done. But then a strange thing happened. Reports of huge tides on the western coast of America came clicking in over the wires. Monstrous tidal waves, the likes of which had never been seen before, were battering the shoreline all along the coast. Violent shock waves were recorded all around the world.

The newsroom was tense with excitement as more reports filtered in. Tidal waves as big as mountains were crashing into many parts of India. Scores of people had died along the shores of the Indian Ocean. At last, reports from ships at sea pointed to the cause—an incredible eruption between Java and Sumatra. An eruption so tremendous, it had destroyed an entire island! The name of the island was *Krakatoa*.

Now a torrent of reports came in: "Volcano erupts on island . . . thousands dead . . . whole island ripped apart . . . monster tidal waves sweep over neighboring islands . . ."

Byron's head reeled. The disaster had occurred at almost exactly the same time he had had his dream!

And in the reports that followed, almost every detail was exactly as he had dreamed it. The incredible fact was that *Byron's nightmare had actually happened.*

Only the name of the island was different. In his dream, Byron had known it as Pralape.

But years later, when Byron had retired, a friend sent him an old map from the Dutch Historical Society. The map was almost two hundred years old, and it showed the island of Krakatoa. But the island wasn't called Krakatoa on the map. It was designated by its original native name, Pralape.

THE
DOOMED PATROL

The pilots of Flight 19 thought they were going on a routine Navy exercise. But a deadly surprise awaited them as they flew into the treacherous territory known as the Bermuda Triangle. . . .

There is a large segment of ocean off the eastern coast of America known as the Bermuda Triangle. It is called this because the area, from midway up the eastern coast across to Bermuda and then down again to the Caribbean Sea and back to Florida, forms a rough triangle on a map.

The Bermuda Triangle happens to be one of the most deadly and mysterious stretches of water in the world. Countless airplanes, boats, and people have disappeared in the area. Without a trace. Without warning. Without explanation.

Pilots have experienced time displacement, seen UFOs, and found themselves over islands that didn't exist. Sailors have seen ghost ships, walls of water a hundred feet high, and weather conditions that were so strange they were almost unearthly.

Into this perilous area, five Navy bombers took off on their last flight on what was to be the most mysterious and talked-about disappearance of aircraft in the annals of aviation.

December 5, 1945. Five Avenger torpedo bombers were about to take off on a routine training mission from the Naval air station at Fort Lauderdale, Florida.

The planes were big, powerful, propeller-driven aircraft with wingspans of over 52 feet. Each plane was to carry a three-man crew, with the exception of the flight leader's bomber, which would carry only two men.

Their flight was designated Flight 19. Their course would take them 160 miles eastward over the ocean, then north for 40 miles, and then back to base on a southwest bearing.

The early-morning skies had been cloudy, but now, at one in the afternoon, the skies had cleared. It was perfect flying weather.

Sergeant Robert Gallivan and Private First Class Robert Gruebel were just leaving their barracks to report to the flight line. They paused to wait for another serviceman, Corporal Allen Kosnar.

But Kosnar called out from his bunk, "You go ahead fellas, I just don't think I'm going to go on that flight."

The two men stared at Kosnar.

"I know, I know," he said. "Sounds nutty, but I just don't feel I want to go. And I don't need to," he added. "I've already done my required flight time for the month, so why should I?"

His friends shrugged and turned to leave. "So long," they said.

"See ya," Kosnar replied.

At 2:02 the first plane took off. The four others followed at one-minute intervals. Six minutes later, Flight 19 was in the air, heading east over the ocean.

There was an old wreck of a cargo ship along their route. When the bombers reached it, the pilots made practice torpedo runs on the ruined hulk. Then the planes regrouped and flew back in formation on their assigned route.

Meanwhile, back at base, Corporal Kosnar spent his time writing a letter to his parents. At 3:45, he looked at his wristwatch. His friends should be landing in about fifteen more minutes.

In the base tower, a radioman also checked his watch. He saw it was almost time for him to go off duty. The afternoon had been uneventful. He stretched and yawned, looking forward to his break.

Suddenly, the radio crackled. A frantic voice came on the airwaves. It was Lieutenant Charles Taylor, the leader of Flight 19.

"Calling tower . . . This is an emergency, tower. *This is an emergency!*"

The radioman sat bolt upright in his chair, suddenly wide-awake.

"This is the tower. Go ahead," he answered.

"We cannot see land. Repeat. *We cannot see land!*" Lieutenant Taylor cried.

The radioman was surprised. How could they not see land? They were supposed to be landing in a few minutes. They should be only about a dozen miles away.

He called back, "What is your position?"

"We are not sure of our position," Taylor answered. "We can't be sure of where we are. We don't know."

Everyone in the tower was astonished. How could these experienced military pilots be lost? They had sophisticated

instruments and the flying knowledge to guide them through practically any situation. Besides, the weather was clear and visibility was excellent.

"Assume bearing due west," the radioman instructed them. If the flight was somewhere east over the ocean, the pilots simply had to head west and they would see land.

But the reply that came back was startling, to say the least.

"We cannot be sure which way is west," Lieutenant Taylor replied. "Everything is wrong . . . strange. Even the ocean doesn't look like it should!"

The personnel in the tower looked at each other in amazement. The sun was near the western horizon. All Flight 19 had to do was to follow the setting sun!

After that last transmission, the tower lost radio contact with the flight. Ten minutes later, the tower heard from Flight 19 again. But instead of asking for more instructions, the crews of the planes were talking among themselves. Flight 19 either could not or would not communicate with the tower. It was evident that the planes were all in sight of one another. It was also evident that everyone on Flight 19 was confused and frightened. The pilots sounded panicked. They disagreed on where they were, which way they should go, and what they should do. They sounded more like a Boy Scout troop lost in the woods than a group of seasoned pilots.

There was no doubt that something strange was happening to them—something that could have no logical explanation.

Then, shortly after four o'clock, the tower personnel heard Lieutenant Taylor turn over command of the flight to another pilot in the group, Marine Captain George Stivers. There was no reason given for this decision, which was extraordinary, to say the least. A commander would turn over his command only if he was no longer able to carry out his duties.

Meanwhile, news of what was happening spread throughout the base like wildfire. When Allen Kosnar heard the report, he raced to the radio tower to hear for himself what was going on.

Just as he entered the room, the voice of Captain Stivers came on the air, addressing the tower. The signal was broken up by a sea of static. Captain Stivers' voice sounded strained and abrupt, like that of a man on the edge of hysteria.

"It is 1625 hours [4:25]. . . . We are not certain where we are. . . . We seem to be lost. We have enough fuel for 75 more minutes. We must be about 225 miles northeast of base . . . looks like we are—"

The message was suddenly cut off. That was the last anyone ever heard from Flight 19.

A massive air and sea search went into effect almost immediately. But nothing was ever found of the lost patrol: no wreckage, no oil slicks, no bits of clothing, not even a scrap of equipment.

Flight 19 had disappeared without a trace.

It was all too incredible. How could five huge planes,

flown by experienced military crews, lose their way at the same time? Especially when all they had to do to find their way back was to follow the sun to the base? Even stranger, why had they lost all sense of direction? Why did things, as Lieutenant Taylor put it, look wrong, strange?

What had happened to them to make them sound so confused and so frightened? All the men were disciplined military fliers. Some of them had even been in combat. They were not the type of men who would panic easily.

One more thing occurred that day to add to the mystery. Two hours after the last plane in the squadron would have run out of fuel, a tower radioman hunched over his set heard the call letters "FT . . . FT . . ." The signal was distant and weak, as if it were coming from thousands of miles away.

The radioman stared at the set in disbelief. "FT" was Flight 19's military call letters! Nobody else would be using them.

Frantically, he tried to make contact, but there was no reply. Even as he searched the airwaves, he knew what he was thinking was impossible. Flight 19 could not still be in the air.

Or could it? Is is possible that Flight 19 *was* still in the air, but in another time and space? A time and space in which everything seemed "wrong" and "strange"?

No one—except the missing airmen of Flight 19—will ever know for sure.

In 1991, a fascinating postscript was added to the mystery of the lost patrol. On May 8 of that year, Graham S. Hawkes, a British undersea explorer, and his crew were exploring the waters off the coast of south Florida, searching for sunken treasure. In the course of their underwater exploration, they stumbled upon five sunken aircraft.

The aircraft were Avenger bombers. The planes were in almost perfect condition, and sitting upright 550 to 750 feet below the surface of the water. One plane was marked "28"—the number stenciled on Flight 19's lead plane. The planes were found in the same general area where the lost squadron had been flying.

Excitement ran high in the media and in aviation circles. The lost patrol had been found!

But after closer examination over the next few weeks, it was discovered that the serial numbers of the aircraft did not match those of Flight 19. Moreover, the planes were slightly older models than the ones flown on Flight 19. The planes could not have belonged to the lost patrol after all.

Of course, this only adds to the mystery. If the five Avenger bombers found by Hawkes were not Flight 19, where did they come from? And what incredible coincidence sent five Avenger bombers to the bottom of the sea in the very area where five other Avenger bombers disappeared off the face of the earth?

THE
ESP DETECTIVE

There have been many cases of psychics who have helped solve crimes. None were more publicized or authenticated than the man they called "The Psychic Detective."

G oing to be lots of bombings—dynamitings! I see two banks blown up and perhaps the city hall. Going to blow up police stations. Then there's going to be a big blow-up south of the river, and then it'll be over."

The person who made these predictions to Detective English of the Milwaukee Police Department on October 18, 1935, was a sixty-nine-year-old man named Arthur Price Roberts. What Arthur was describing seemed to be a series of terrorist bombings. The Milwaukee police did not take this information lightly. Arthur was already well known as a "psychic detective." Throughout his life he had made many predictions that had come true. He had also helped solve a number of crimes in the past. The police, therefore, decided to take extra precautions and increase their patrols of the city.

In spite of their care, the first of the bombings occurred eight days later in suburban Shorewood, killing two children and injuring scores of others. Then, on October 27, two Milwaukee banks were blown up. This was quickly followed by the bombings of two police stations. So far, everything was happening as Arthur had predicted. If there had been any lingering doubts about his strange ability, these events erased them.

Detective English and his superior officers quickly contacted Arthur and asked him what they should expect next.

"On Sunday, November fourth, there'll be a big one south of the river," he told them. "And that'll be all."

Sure enough, on the afternoon of Sunday, November 4, a thunderous explosion ripped through a garage in a section of the city known as the Menomonee District. The explosion was so huge that people as far way as eight miles heard the sound. Crowds rushed into the streets to see what had happened.

All the police found on the scene were the grisly and scattered remains of two bodies. The garage itself was totally destroyed. But after a painstaking investigation, the police were able to identify the two victims who had been in the garage when it had exploded. They turned out to be the terrorists themselves! It seemed they had been fashioning their latest bomb out of fifty pounds of dynamite when it accidentally detonated.

Just as Arthur had predicted, the explosion was indeed the last of the bombings.

If that case's outcome had seemed uncanny to others, it was no more than a familiar story for Arthur Price Roberts. He had had the ability to locate missing persons and objects and to "see" into the future ever since he had been a child growing up in England.

Oddly enough, Arthur could not read. He was afraid to learn, believing that if he did, he might destroy his strange ability.

Throughout his life, as news of his incredible feats spread, Arthur kept mementos of his successes. They spanned a period of fifty years.

Occasionally, Arthur worked with people in the role of a private detective. One case involved a woman whose husband had disappeared. Duncan McGregor, of Peshtigo, in northeastern Wisconsin, had suddenly vanished one day. Countless false clues had been followed, and generous rewards had been offered, but months later, there was still no trace of the missing man. In desperation, Mrs. McGregor came to see Arthur personally to ask for his help.

Arthur had never met her or heard of her problem, yet when he opened the door of his home in Milwaukee, he immediately knew who she was and why she was there. Arthur told her to come back in a few hours so that he could think about the case.

When Mrs. McGregor returned later that afternoon, she received some tragic news. Arthur told her that her husband had been murdered. "But," he added, "I cannot tell you who was responsible for his death. The testimony I could give you would not be admissible evidence in court." Arthur *was* able to tell Mrs. McGregor where her husband's body could be found. It was at the bottom of the Menominee River, he said. It was unable to rise to the surface because it was snagged on sunken logs.

Mrs. McGregor took this information to the police, who searched the spot that Arthur had described. Soon, they brought up the body of the missing man. McGregor's clothing had indeed been tangled in sunken logs, just as Arthur had stated!

Along with his powers of ESP, Arthur seemed to possess a kind of mental radar. When a taxi driver named Fred Kores was mugged and thrown out of his car, Warren Boucher, the owner of the cab company, asked Arthur to help find the stolen cab.

Twenty-four hours later, Arthur barged into Warren Boucher's office. "I've located your car," he cried. "But you'll have to hurry before the thief gets away!" Arthur, Warren, Fred, and a friend scrambled into Warren's car and sped off. Arthur excitedly gave them directions as if he were following a radio signal.

"This way—no, that way!"

"Down this road!"

"Keep on going along here."

Warren maneuvered the car this way and that, trying to keep pace with Arthur's instructions.

Finally they came to an intersection on the road to Chicago. Instead of giving further directions, Arthur asked Warren to stop the car until he got his bearings. He left the car, pacing nervously back and forth like a bloodhound off its scent. Suddenly he jumped back into the car, pointed down a side road, and cried, "Go that way!"

The car had gone no more than a quarter of a mile down the side road when Arthur shouted, "The car is coming toward us! Turn around and we'll follow it!"

Just then, the men saw several cars approaching, all moving fast. Warren swerved the car off to the side of the road and waited. A few seconds later, a taxi whizzed by on the lane opposite. They could all see the driver clearly.

"That's it," Fred Kores yelled. "That's my cab and that's the guy who slugged me!"

Warren quickly pulled into the lane and followed the cab. They managed to force it off the road. The four men got out and seized the driver. A few hours later, the Milwaukee police had the man in custody. The man confessed to committing the crime.

Arthur Price Roberts had done it again!

Arthur could apply his psychic abilities to his own life as well. After attending a dinner party in his honor in November of 1939, Arthur told the group, "You know how I enjoy these meetings of ours, but I am afraid I won't be present at the next one you are talking about. As much as I would like to remain, I won't be with you beyond January 2, 1940."

That sad prediction turned out to be as accurate as all his others had been. Several weeks later, Arthur died quietly in his home, surrounded by file cabinets containing records of his remarkable achievements.

The date was January 2, 1940.

THE WEEPING STATUE

A three-hundred-year-old statue rested in its niche in an old church. There was nothing remarkable about it . . . until the day it started to cry.

On May 13, 1957, a startling report came from the tiny village of Rocca Corneta in Italy. It was said that a wooden statue in the local church was weeping human tears.

The statue was a life-sized Madonna that had been carved in the seventeenth century. For years, it had held a place of honor in the village church. Now that this remarkable event had occurred, the incident was immediately proclaimed a divine miracle.

The first ones to witness this strange event were the villagers themselves. They were simple people, with a strong belief in God and the supernatural. The religious authorities in Rome, however, were not so easily convinced. Not content with the word of superstitious farmers and laborers, they had samples of the tears taken from the statue and brought to Rome to be analyzed. Two scientists at the police pathological laboratories there conducted a thorough series of tests. When they were finished, they returned to a room where three priests and some newspaper reporters were waiting.

The scientists delivered their findings. "The liquid we have analyzed has all the characteristics of human tears."

The priests and reporters greeted the news with astonishment. How could this be possible?

After the report was made public, there were many who still thought it *wasn't* possible. It was just a clever trick, these people argued. Perhaps it was a scheme to turn the vil-

lage into a tourist attraction. So in 1960, a special church commission went to Rocca Corneta to get to the bottom of the "Weeping Madonna" mystery.

The first thing the commission did was to take the statue down and have it X-rayed. The X rays showed there was nothing inside. The statue was solid wood.

So far, no tears had appeared. The commission was beginning to doubt that any would. Nonetheless, they mounted an around-the-clock vigil on the statue and locked up the church to make sure that no one but the members of the commission could enter it. The statue itself was placed in a double-locked glass case that stood a few feet off the ground, on a platform away from any of the church walls. As an added precaution, the case was brightly lit by powerful floodlights. The church authorities were now satisfied that no one could "fake" the tears without their knowing it.

For a while it seemed as if the nonbelievers were right. For six days, the statue remained dry-eyed. Then, on the seventh day, the priest on duty noticed a bit of moisture around the statue's eyes. Two movie cameras had been set up near the statue. The priest quickly turned them on. Seconds later, what appeared to be tears began coursing down the dark wooden cheeks of the Madonna.

For fifteen minutes the tears fell as the close-up cameras whirred away in the hushed silence of the old church. Then, as suddenly as they had started, the tears stopped. But now the event had been recorded on film.

Despite the evidence, there were still people who believed there was a rational explanation for the "miracle." Arguments raged back and forth between the believers and the nonbelievers.

The church authorities didn't know what to make of it all. The tears were there—that much was obvious. But what caused them? In spite of findings from the original analysis, was there any way the tears could be made of wood sap? In 1962, the church invited an expert on antique wood to conduct tests on the statue.

The expert's conclusion? Far from being able to produce sap, the three-hundred-year-old wood was actually full of dry rot. There wasn't a drop of moisture in the entire statue!

For three years, the riddle of the statue continued to puzzle experts and ordinary people alike. In 1965, another church commission was set up to examine the statue. This time, the commission took the statue out of the church and placed it in the strong room of a local bank. As before, the statue was placed in a glass case. The only people with keys to the vault were the members of the church commission, who were also the only ones allowed to enter.

To the amazement of all, the Madonna continued to weep—sometimes up to two hours at a time!

By this time, more than one hundred authenticated instances of the weeping had been recorded. The church had no explanation for the phenomenon. Neither did anyone else.

When someone asked Father Dante Chelli, the parish priest in Rocca Corneta, what he thought of it all, he said, "That she weeps is beyond question. Why and how are beyond the understanding of a poor prelate."

Is it truly a miracle, or is it some fantastic freak of nature? Either way, it is a mystery that seems likely never to be solved.

CAPTURED BY ALIENS!

You probably don't believe in flying saucers or creatures from outer space. Neither did Betty and Barney Hill of Portsmouth, New Hampshire. But one clear and starry night, on a lonely New Hampshire road, something happened that changed their minds forever. . . .

etty and Barney Hill lived in Portsmouth, New Hampshire. No one would ever have heard of them if it weren't for the fact that they claimed they were kidnapped by aliens and taken aboard their spaceship!

The Hills were an ordinary, down-to-earth couple, not given to flights of fancy or wild imaginings. Barney had a job with the United States Civil Rights Commission and Betty was a social worker for the state of New Hampshire.

On the evening of September 19, 1961, the Hills were driving on U.S. 3, on the last leg of their journey home after a vacation trip to Canada. Their dachshund, Delsey, was lying snugly between them on the floor. Barney was alert and driving carefully because the road cut through deep mountain gorges and was dark and full of twists and turns.

It was a few minutes before eleven o'clock, and at that time of night, the highway was completely deserted. The Hills began to feel nervous. What if they had a breakdown or some other emergency? They might be stranded for hours.

Suddenly, a strange flying object loomed before them in the night sky.

Barney and Betty watched the object with growing wonder and fear as it kept pace with their car. It seemed to be following them. After a few minutes, it picked up speed, changed course, and suddenly came directly toward them.

Barney braked sharply and swung the car into a nearby picnic area at the side of the road. They both got out, with

Delsey waddling close behind, and stood in the picnic area. The craft had slowed down when they had stopped and was now hovering in the distance.

Barney was puzzled. When they had first seen the flying object, he had insisted to Betty that it had to be a commercial airliner or a small private plane. Now he raised a pair of binoculars he had taken out of the car to get a better look. The aircraft looked like the fuselage of a plane, but it had no wings. A series of flashing colored lights ran along its side.

Barney shook his head. "It's *got* to be a plane," he said. "Maybe a military plane. A search plane. Maybe it's a plane that's lost." Barney shook his head again as Delsey whined and cowered behind him.

"Let me see," Betty said, taking the binoculars from her husband.

At that moment, the object passed in front of the full moon. Betty saw what looked like thin pencils of different colored lights flashing from the object.

She gasped. It had to be a real flying saucer.

Confused and excited, she thrust the binoculars back at Barney, swept Delsey up into her arms, dashed back into the car, and slammed the door shut.

Barney hurried to join her. In no time, he started the car and drove back onto the highway. As they roared down the road, the Hills looked nervously up over their shoulders, hoping they would see nothing but empty sky. But the spaceship was following them!

Barney insisted that the craft was a plane of some sort and tried to ignore it. Betty was exasperated.

"Barney, I don't know *why* you're trying not to look at this," she cried. "Stop again and look at it!"

"It'll go away by the time I do that," Barney answered. But he stopped the car once more and got out.

For the first time, he saw the object close up. It was no more than a short city block away from him. It hovered just above the treetops, looking like a glowing pancake hanging in the air, with a double row of windows around its rim.

Now Barney felt scared. There was no doubt about it. This was no plane. It really *was* an alien spaceship! But for some reason he couldn't understand, he started to walk toward the object. Betty screamed after him to stop. But Barney kept on going, cutting across a field. Soon he disappeared from sight.

A short time later, just as Betty was about to panic completely, she heard a scream. It was Barney! He pounded up to the car, nearly hysterical, and jumped into the driver's seat. He slammed the car into first gear and shot off down the road, shouting to Betty that he was sure they were about to be captured.

That was the last clear memory either of them had about the drive for some time. Barney and Betty suddenly fell into a dreamlike stupor as the car sped along. The next thing they knew, they were nearing a sign that read Concord—17 Miles. It was at that moment that they suddenly felt fully awake again.

Barney and Betty weren't sure what had happened to them. But when they got home at last, Barney looked at his watch. The drive home had taken two hours longer than it should have. Somehow, they had lost two hours of time—and couldn't account for what had taken place during that interval. They were sure they hadn't spent two hours looking at the strange spaceship.

Ten days after the sighting, Betty began to have strange nightmares—nightmares about being brought aboard a spaceship and examined by aliens! The dreams were very upsetting. They were so vivid, Betty felt as if she were dreaming about something that had actually happened. Barney too was depressed and worried, but he couldn't put his finger on what was bothering him. All he knew was that he had felt uneasy since the night he had seen the spaceship.

The Hills decided to undergo hypnosis by Dr. Benjamin Simon, a well-known scientist. They both felt the key to their odd behavior lay in the events that had occurred during those two missing hours. Perhaps hypnosis would help them remember.

What was revealed under hypnosis was incredible! After Barney had gotten into the car the second time, the Hills had driven down the road, only to find their way blocked by a group of strange-looking men who were standing right in the middle of the highway. Barney screeched the car to a halt, and he and Betty got out. The group of men approached them, and the Hills felt powerless to run or resist, as if they were held in some sort of trance.

The men took them to the UFO, which had landed in a clearing, and forced the Hills to go in.

Barney described what he saw inside: "The interior of the craft was filled with a bluish light," he said, "and by that I mean a fluorescent kind of light that didn't cast any shadows. And I could see the curved contour of the corridor."

Then he went on to describe their captors. The aliens had oval-shaped heads with large slanting eyes that wrapped around their faces. Their mouths seemed to have no muscle, but were just slits above their chins.

The aliens examined Betty and Barney as if they were lab specimens. They were firm but not rough with the Hills. They even talked to Betty and Barney from time to time. Strangely enough, the Hills could understand every word of what the aliens were saying, although they had no idea how they could do so. The Hills later came to believe that the aliens used a kind of mind contact, rather than speech, to communicate.

Betty remembered them inserting a needle into her abdomen. When she asked her captors what they were doing, they answered that it was a pregnancy test. At that time, no such test was ever used in connection with a pregnancy. Today, it is a widely used procedure, used to determine the health of a baby before it is born.

Betty was also shown a star map by the aliens, who told her it showed their expedition routes. Betty, who had no knowledge of astronomy, later drew the map from memory. A year later, a very similar star map was published in *The New York Times* as part of a scientific article.

As unbelievable as the Hills' story seems, Dr. Simon and the other scientists familiar with the case agreed that the Hills were not faking. There was no way they could have made up such an elaborate story together. Betty and Barney were hypnotized separately. They each told basically the same story, although naturally from their own points of view.

The overwhelming opinion of the scientists investigating the case was that Betty and Barney were telling the absolute truth!

A book has been written about their experiences. The story of their ordeal has even been made into a TV movie.

Were Betty and Barney Hill captured by aliens? All in all, it seems that that is a very real possibility. And if that is so, it would be the first face-to-face encounter with beings from another world ever recorded!

THE GHOST CAVALRY

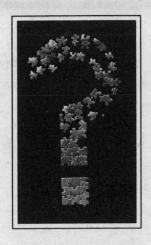

On April 24, 1940, a strange story appeared in an English publication, The National Message.

The story was told firsthand by a highly trained observer, Captain Cecil Wightmick Haywood. It is one of the most astounding tales to come out of World War I.

I t was the year 1918. England and its allies were fighting a world war with Germany. All of Europe had become a bloody battleground.

One of the many front lines scattered across the continent was called the "La Bassée" front, after the canal that flowed along its length. The La Bassée Canal was located near the small Belgian town of Béthune, which was in Allied hands. Since Béthune was just behind the front lines, it was in a strategic location. Troops constantly marched in and out of the small village on their way to and from the front.

It was here that Captain Haywood was stationed. He was a staff captain with First Corps British Intelligence, and his job was to gather as much information as he could about the strength and positions of the German troops along the front.

In the early part of 1918, the situation at La Bassée was getting desperate. The Germans were steadily advancing. The Allies were suffering heavy losses. To stem the advance, Portuguese troops were sent to shore up the defenses. But on the day these troops took up their positions, the Germans gave them a terrific pounding with their big guns. It wasn't long before the Portuguese soldiers fled, leaving a wide gap in the Allied lines.

A massive German attack now seemed inevitable. As a delaying tactic, British machine gunners were quickly set up along the banks of the La Bassée Canal, facing the German line. Captain Haywood accompanied the troops.

The British soldiers were tense and alert as they grimly waited for the Germans to attack once again with their big guns. The men didn't have long to wait. Soon, the terrifying high-pitched screech of flying shells echoed through the air, followed by the thumps and crunch of explosions as the missiles crashed into the ground around them.

Captain Haywood and the rest of his men hugged the ground for dear life. At any moment, they expected the Germans to break through their thin line of defense.

But suddenly, the Germans turned their fire on a barren patch of ground near the town. From his position, Captain Haywood could see puffs of black smoke and flashes of explosions as one shell after another pounded the desolate area. Then German machine gunners opened up and raked the same area with machine gun fire.

The British soldiers watched these maneuvers in astonishment. Captain Haywood was mystified. There were no troops or equipment there. The area was totally deserted. Why were the Germans hitting it?

As if to echo his thoughts, a British sergeant crouching next to him cried out, "The Germans have gone balmy, sir! Why in the world are they directing their fire on that open ground?"

Captain Haywood slowly shook his head. "I haven't the faintest idea," he replied.

To add to the mystery, the firing stopped as abruptly as

it had begun. Moments later, a deathly silence fell over the field of battle.

Cautiously, the captain crept up to a ridge on the bank of the canal and peered over the top of it.

A scene of utter chaos met his eyes. The German troops were in complete disarray. Masses of soldiers were retreating in confusion and panic, throwing away weapons and supplies in their desperation to get away.

Captain Haywood was amazed. Why were tough, disciplined troops fleeing the battlefield like frightened schoolboys?

The incredible answer came a few days later, when Haywood questioned some captured German officers.

It seemed that the Germans had been about to advance, confident of victory, when suddenly they spied a formation of ghostly cavalry on a hill near Béthune. The sight had been unsettling, to say the least.

"They were all clad in white, and mounted on white horses," an officer recalled.

All the Germans had seen them, including the spotters for the artillery. It was then that the order to open fire had been given. The artillery and machine guns had chewed up that patch of ground. The Germans said the firepower had been fierce. They had seen many shells and bullets hit their targets. But not one white horseman fell!

"The cavalry rode quietly forward at a slow trot," another officer stated. "In front of them rode their leader—a fine figure of a man; by his side was a great sword, not a cavalry sword, but similar to those used by the Crusaders. And in his hands lay quietly the reins of his white charger."

The ghost riders calmly rode through the murderous fire until they were not more than a hundred yards from the German lines. It was then that the German troops had retreated in fear and panic—just as victory had been in their grasp. Just when nothing had stood in their way but a few machine guns!

No one had an explanation for the strange occurrence. The British troops had not seen it, and as far as they were concerned, no such cavalry existed.

But to the Germans, watching fearfully from the other side, the ghostly horsemen had been terrifyingly real.

It is unlikely that an entire army imagined the whole thing. And yet, what *did* happen that fateful day? No one had the answer then, and no one does now.

PORTRAITS OF DEATH

André Marcellin's portraits were so
amazing that they thrilled their
subjects . . . to death.

André Marcellin was a French artist who began his career in Paris in 1907. Although he is not well known today, in his time he was famous as a gifted painter of landscapes. But his real talent was in painting portraits.

There was one odd thing about André's portraits. Almost all of them were pictures of people who were already dead. In fact, André said that he would rather paint dead subjects than live ones.

This preference puzzled André's friends. They believed that painting portraits of living people would help André's career as an artist, and they encouraged him to take on such work whenever possible.

At last, one day, a wealthy French businessman talked André into doing his portrait. Although André was reluctant, he began the painting. After a few weeks it was finished. André did not seem happy with it, but the businessman was pleased.

Two days after the picture was finished, the businessman suddenly died.

André was very upset by the news. His friends were quick to point out that the man's death was a sad coincidence that couldn't have anything to do with the portrait. But André had a strange feeling that there was more to it than that.

Nevertheless, six months later, he was talked into doing another portrait.

A few days after that painting was finished, its subject died suddenly.

André was convinced that there was a connection between his portraits and the sudden deaths. He vowed never again to do portraits of living people. The next time he was asked to paint a portrait, he refused. The client angrily demanded to know why.

André finally told him. "I always had a strange reluctance to paint portraits from life. It was a feeling I did not quite understand," he said. "Then, some time ago, I agreed with great reluctance to paint two of them. Both sitters died suddenly, immediately after the portraits were completed."

The client insisted that the deaths were just a coincidence.

André didn't agree. "I am quite certain there is a curse on my portrait work," he said. "Whomever I paint is doomed to die soon afterward."

But the client insisted that André was wrong. The idea of a curse was ridiculous, he argued. "Now, if that is your only reason for not painting my portrait," he said, "when do we start?"

André sighed. Because the man would not give up, André finally agreed to do the work. With many misgivings, he began. When the picture was finished, the client was delighted. It was one of André's best paintings.

Three days later, the man died as suddenly and as unexpectedly as the other sitters.

Now whispered rumors about André's paintings began to circulate. In addition to the three deaths, there was this odd story: In 1912, a fire destroyed a home in Turin, Italy, killing four people. The only painting left untouched by the flames in the room where the fire had started was André's portrait of St. Christopher.

In the spring of 1913 André became engaged to a pretty girl named Françoise Noël. Françoise had heard of his skill as a portrait painter, but had not heard the rumors about his work. She asked André to paint her. The artist refused without telling her why.

Françoise was offended. She believed that André did not think she was interesting enough to paint.

One day she gave him an ultimatum. If he didn't paint her, she would not marry him.

André was forced to tell her the truth about his paintings. "There is a curse upon me," he said. "I must never paint a portrait again. I am mortally afraid—afraid that if I painted your portrait, then soon you would die; and what would there be left in life for me then?"

But like the other sitters before her, Françoise did not believe there was a curse on the paintings. For months, she begged André to paint her.

At last André gave in. He started her portrait in October 1913.

A week later, Françoise died.

André became a broken man. He was inconsolable. He

felt that life without Françoise was no longer worth living. One day he made a fateful decision: He would paint himself!

André worked for days, putting all the skill he possessed into the self-portrait. The painting turned out to be his masterpiece. It was also the last picture he would ever paint.

Four days later, on January 2, 1914, André Marcellin died.

But the curse did not die with him. In May of 1966, one of André's paintings came up for auction in Milan. Bidding was slow, but the picture was finally sold to a businessman from Rome. The man took it home and hung it in his study.

A few weeks later, the businessman and his wife were dead.

There are a total of twenty Marcellin portraits scattered around the world. No one knows where all the pictures are. But no one who knows the history of the curse is anxious to locate them, either.

THE TEENAGER WHO SAW HER OWN FUTURE

Most people say they would like to see the future. But sometimes, as in the case of a teenager named Anna, it's better not to know what's in store for you. Anna's incredible story has been recorded and witnessed by two of the most gifted psychiatrists in America.

It all began on the morning of September 19, 1949, when a seventeen-year-old girl named Anna Walmsley arrived at the Department of Psychiatry in a famous eastern university's medical school.

Anna had agreed to be the "guinea pig" in an experiment dealing with time. The psychiatrists who were conducting the experiment, Dr. Lohman and Dr. Stanley, wanted to find out if someone could see into the future while under hypnosis. They knew that some people had the ability to predict events before they actually happened. But these same people had no idea how they did it. The doctors believed that the phenomenon was connected to self-hypnosis, and wanted to see if they could somehow duplicate the process under laboratory conditions.

As the experiment began, the two scientists put Anna into a trance. When Anna was deeply and completely under hypnosis, the doctors urged her to project her mind into the future.

Anna's brow furrowed in concentration as she tried to do as the doctors asked. Suddenly, her expression changed. Her face screwed up in pain. Tears streamed from her eyes and she began to sob. She shuddered as she tried to control her anguish. At last she gave up.

"My baby, my baby!" she cried in a pitiful voice. "My baby is dead!" She rocked back and forth, repeating these words over and over.

The two doctors looked at each other with alarm. The

experiment was getting out of control. They brought Anna out of her trance immediately.

When she regained full consciousness, she was very frightened. Dr. Lohman asked her what she had seen.

"It was about half past three one afternoon," Anna said in a quivering voice. "I—I was married and I was standing close to a cradle. In the cradle lay a young baby—it was *my* baby . . . and he was dead!"

She turned her worried face to the two scientists. "Do you think it will really happen that way?" she asked. "Do you think I will have a baby who will die?"

Both doctors realized that something had gone terribly wrong with the experiment. Nevertheless, they tried to assure Anna that everything was all right. It was extremely unlikely that what she had seen would really happen in the future, they told her. But Anna didn't seem convinced. She was very upset now, and both men felt responsible.

Dr. Stanley patted her on the shoulder.

"Go home and forget about it," he said soothingly. "This was nothing more than an experiment."

It was true. The scientists had no way of knowing if Anna's dream was anything more than just that—a dream. After all, how could they prove that Anna had seen into the future? It was very possible she had invented the scene out of her imagination, from her fears and anxieties.

Still, the doctors recorded everything that had happened as part of their ongoing research.

Years passed as Dr. Lohman and Dr. Stanley continued their experiments, using other volunteers. They were still looking for proof that someone could see into the future under hypnosis. They hadn't found it yet.

But the doctors kept careful records of the lives of all their volunteers. When Anna got married in 1953, it was noted in her file. When she gave birth to a baby boy in July 1954, they recorded that event as well.

In September of the same year, something odd happened. Dr. Stanley was struck with an overwhelming urge to visit Anna and her husband. He had no idea why he was feeling this way; he only knew he had to see her. So he left his office and drove to her house.

It was early evening by the time he arrived. And when he did, he found Anna and her husband grief-stricken.

Dr. Stanley immediately asked what had happened. Anna told him. Early that afternoon, their baby had suddenly become ill. At half past three, the child had died in his cradle.

Dr. Stanley was thunderstruck. The event was exactly what Anna had foreseen under hypnosis, even down to the time of death!

The long-ago experiment had been a success after all. Anna Walmsley had actually seen into the future—her future, tragic as it turned out to be.

A GHOSTLY
SUMMONS

One of the most famous doctors during the latter part of the nineteenth
century, *Dr. S. Weir Mitchell of
Philadelphia, related this true incident
of what happened to him one stormy
night in December.*

It was ten thirty at night. Large snowflakes, like fluffy white feathers, were drifting down upon the city of Philadelphia. The weather and the freezing temperature kept most people indoors. The snow-covered streets were empty and cold.

Dr. Mitchell let out a sigh of relief as the last patient left his office. It had been a long and tiring day. He dimmed the gaslight in his consulting room and trudged wearily upstairs to bed.

Half an hour later, just as he was about to fall asleep, his doorbell rang. The doctor opened his eyes and groaned. He hoped he had just imagined the sound. But the bell jangled again. There was no doubt someone was at the door.

Dr. Mitchell struggled into his robe and slippers. As tired as he was, he was a dedicated doctor. The call might be an emergency. He made his way downstairs to the front door.

A small young girl was standing on the doorstep amid a swirl of snowflakes. She was wearing no coat in the frigid weather, just a green woolen dress over her too-thin body. A flimsy gray-plaid shawl covered her head, while a shabby pair of high-button shoes encased her feet.

Dr. Mitchell guessed that she was from the poor side of town, a few blocks away. He gazed kindly at the girl. "Won't you come in out of the snow, please?"

The girl nodded and stepped just inside the door. "My mother is very sick," she said. "She needs you right away, sir. Please come with me." Although her manner was timid and polite, there was a look of determination on her pinched face.

The doctor raised his eyebrows in surprise. The girl was a total stranger. She was asking him to give up his warm bed and race off to an unknown destination in the middle of the night—in a snowstorm, no less.

"Don't you have a family doctor, young lady?" he asked.

The girl shook her head so urgently that snow fell from her shawl. "No, sir. And my mother is dreadfully ill," she answered. "Please come with me! Please do! Now!"

The doctor could see tears welling up in the girl's eyes. He didn't have the heart to refuse her. "Very well," he said, "but please be seated while I dress."

"I would rather stand here," the girl answered.

Dr. Mitchell nodded and hurried upstairs. A short time later, he and the girl were trudging through the snowy streets. Dr. Mitchell realized that his earlier guess about the girl's home had been correct. They were heading for the poorest section of town. Here, factory workers and day laborers lived from hand to mouth, never knowing if they would have enough money to last out the week until the next payday. Those who had no jobs were even worse off. It was a place where starvation and despair were all too common.

The doctor himself was no stranger to the neighborhood. He had made many visits to patients in the area, despite the fact that few could pay him for his efforts.

Dr. Mitchell observed that his companion was unnaturally quiet. She walked a few steps in front of him, and never once looked back or said a word.

At last she turned into a narrow alley between two run-down tenements. They entered one of the houses, and the girl felt her way up a dark stairway. The doctor followed close behind. As they approached her apartment, he could see the weak light of an oil lamp coming from the door, which stood ajar. The girl gently pushed the door open and silently stood aside to let him enter.

Dr. Mitchell looked around the room in dismay. A threadbare carpet covered the center of the splintery wooden floor. A tin cupboard stood in one corner of the room, next to an old iron stove with no fire in it. A middle-aged woman was lying in a bed near the stove, struggling for breath.

Dr. Mitchell immediately examined her. The woman had pneumonia. She was very, very ill, as her daughter had said. But the doctor knew he had gotten there in time to save her. The first thing that had to be done was to get the patient warm. The doctor turned to ask the girl to build a fire. But she was gone.

Dr. Mitchell looked around in surprise, wondering where she was. The open door of a small, rickety clothes cabinet caught his eye. Inside the cabinet were a familiar-looking woolen dress, plaid shawl, and high-button shoes—

clothes the girl had been wearing only minutes before.

How could she have changed so quickly? the doctor wondered. And how had he not seen her do so? The one-room apartment was very small. He touched the clothes in the cabinet. They were completely dry!

The doctor looked back at the woman lying in bed. She was watching him with a sorrowful expression on her face.

"Those are my daughter's clothes," the woman said. She spoke as if every breath were causing her pain.

The doctor nodded. "I know," he said. "But where is she? I have to talk to her."

The woman looked at him in bewilderment. There was a long, painful silence. At last she spoke.

"Talk to her?" she said, tears coming to her eyes. "Doctor, my daughter died two months ago!"

Dr. Mitchell was speechless. Never in all his years of practice had something like this happened. He had not imagined the girl, that was certain. And he had not imagined the clothes she'd been wearing either.

Impossible as it seemed, there was no other explanation. He had been led to the woman's bedside by the ghost of her dead daughter!

THE BULLET
WITH A MEMORY

The following story might be an example of an incredible coincidence. On the other hand, it might be an example of something beyond our understanding.

It was a hot day in 1893 when Henry Ziegland jilted his sweetheart in the small, dusty town of Honey Grove, Texas. That would have been the end of a sad, familiar story if it hadn't been for the fact that Henry's sweetheart committed suicide shortly thereafter.

The girl's enraged brother, bent on revenge, took his gun and went looking for the man whom he blamed for his sister's tragic death. Henry, who had no idea that his life was in danger, went about his daily chores as usual. When his sweetheart's brother found him, he was standing by a tree in his pasture.

The brother immediately fired. Henry fell to the ground, blood pouring from his face. The killer ran from the scene, sure that Henry was dead.

But soon, remorse over both his sister's death and the murder he had just committed overcame him. A few hours later, he too committed suicide.

Henry, however, hadn't been killed after all. The bullet had just grazed his head, causing a great deal of blood to flow. The force of the blow had knocked him out. He had fallen to the ground as if he were dead. The bullet, meanwhile, had buried itself in the thick trunk of the tree behind him.

By a stroke of luck, Henry Ziegland's life had been spared.

Through the years, the memory of that fateful day slowly faded until it was almost completely forgotten.

One day in 1913, twenty years after the incident, Henry decided to cut down a tree in his pasture. It turned out to be a tougher job than he expected. After laboring over the task for many hours, he decided to use dynamite to speed the process.

He fused the dynamite and placed it in the tree. Then, walking a safe distance away, he waited for the explosion. It came a few moments later, but it was the last sound that he ever heard. The tree that Henry had been attempting to cut down was the tree with the bullet in its trunk. And as the tree exploded, the bullet lodged deep inside came flying out with tremendous force.

That same bullet, aimed at his head twenty years earlier by a vengeful brother, finally found its mark and killed Henry instantly!

THE HUMAN CORK

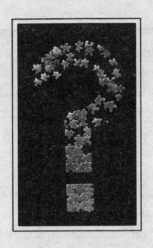

He was called *"The Man They Couldn't Drown." And amazingly enough, it was true!*

A ngelo Faticoni was an ordinary enough man with one outstanding ability. He floated.

Angelo could do things in the water that no one else could. He could sleep on the surface, roll himself up into a ball, or take any other position that was asked of him, all without sinking!

His feats became so famous that he was known as "The Human Cork."

Once Angelo was even sewn into a canvas bag, with a twenty-pound cannonball tied to his legs. Soon after being put in water, his head appeared on the surface, his body free of the bag. The twenty-pound cannonball was still tied securely in place. He remained that way for eight hours.

Angelo even went to Harvard to perform for the students and faculty there. Like everyone else, they were amazed by his fantastic ability.

Angelo believed that he was able to float for such great lengths of time because of the peculiar nature of his internal organs. He underwent numerous tests by medical authorities, but no basis was ever found for this claim.

When Angelo Faticoni died on August 2, 1931, he was so well known that the *New York Herald Tribune* noted the event. During his lifetime, Angelo often promised that someday he would reveal his secret. But he never did.

THE HAUNTED SUBMARINE

Many strange tales are told about the
sea and those who sail on it. But none
is stranger than the story of U-boat
65. . . .

U-boat 65 was a brand-new submarine that had just been commissioned by the German Navy. And on a stormy September day in 1916, it went out on its first test run.

The sea was choppy and the boat bucked and rolled as its bow cut a foamy path through the gray water. The crew's mood seemed to match the weather. It had been rumored that five workmen had been killed during the boat's construction—a sure sign to the superstitious seamen that the ship might be unlucky.

Before the first test dive, the captain ordered a petty officer to inspect the hull to make sure everything was secure. The young man calmly climbed down from the conning tower, a narrow enclosed platform perched above the sub's hull, and strolled along the top deck. Then, without a word of warning, he jumped overboard! He was never seen again.

In minutes, the news of this event spread throughout the sub. To the already anxious crew, it could only mean one thing—the ship was jinxed!

The captain also seemed to be shaken by the bizarre event, but he ordered the test dive to go on. The crew snapped into action. Soon water gurgled along the hull of *UB-65* as it started to sink beneath the sea. At thirty-five feet, the captain gave the order to level out. But the submarine kept diving.

The crew tried desperately to remedy the situation. All efforts were useless. *UB-65* continued to sink. At last, it stopped—but not before it had come to rest on the bottom of the sea.

For fifteen agonizing hours, the sub wallowed helplessly on the ocean floor. The water pressure at that depth was too much for the fragile hull, and its riveted plates began to buckle under the strain. From numerous cracks in the hull, seawater slowly seeped into the sub. To make matters worse, the oxygen supply was dwindling. It was becoming hard for the men to breathe.

Just when the crew thought the end was near, *UB-65* suddenly floated upward of its own accord. After this near-disaster, the ship headed back to port with a very worried captain and crew.

Their worry was well founded. There was still more bad luck to come.

While *UB-65* was safely docked and taking on supplies, a torpedo being hauled aboard blew up, killing the first lieutenant and five enlisted men. Because of the damage, the submarine had to stay in port for repairs. The crew was given shore leave. Only a handful of men stayed on board.

That night, aboard the sub, a petty officer stumbled into the captain's cabin.

"I saw it! It's come aboard," he screamed. "The ghost of the first lieutenant!"

The captain followed the petty officer on deck. At the bow he could make out a figure of a man dressed in the uniform of a first lieutenant. He was standing with his back to them and looking out to sea. Then, as the two stared in disbelief, the man disappeared!

Now both the captain and his crew were convinced that the submarine was haunted as well as jinxed. But they had no choice but to go back to sea. It was 1916, and a world war was in progress. It was their duty as German sailors to help serve their country.

For the next few months, everything went well. The U-boat even sank a few enemy ships. The relieved crew began to think their luck had changed for the better.

Then one day, after a grueling underwater patrol, the captain decided to surface and give his men the luxury of breathing some fresh air. Seconds after surfacing, the lookout in the conning tower shouted, "It's come back! It's standing there with its arms folded, just like the petty officer said!"

From inside the sub's control room, the captain scrambled up the tower. When he got to the top, he looked to the bow where the lookout was pointing. The ghost was there again!

It was dressed in a first lieutenant's uniform, and had its back to him. Its arms appeared to be folded across its chest.

The captain told himself to keep calm. He climbed down the conning tower ladder to the top deck.

"Who are you?" he called out.

At the captain's cry, the thing at the bow slowly turned around. For the first time the captain saw its face. It was the first lieutenant who had been killed in the torpedo explosion!

The captain staggered back. Before he could do or say anything else, the figure faded away before his eyes.

There was no doubt that *UB-65* was still haunted. The captain and crew were badly shaken, and the submarine immediately headed back to base.

News of the haunted sub had reached the German High Command. When the sub reached base, a chaplain came on board to perform an exorcism. Then *UB-65* was sent back to sea. The captain and crew hoped the exorcism had worked.

But the jinx continued. A few days after leaving base, the leading gunner went mad and killed himself. The next day, at dawn, one of the petty officers jumped overboard and sank beneath the waves. Both men had claimed to have seen the ghost in the preceding twenty-four hours.

Once more, *UB-65* headed back to base.

The sailors were so rattled, the German High Command decided to outfit the sub with a fresh crew. And so it was that when *UB-65* sailed out of port and headed for the southern tip of Ireland, it carried a brand-new crew.

If that crew experienced the same things the previous one had, no one will ever know. Because not one of those sailors was ever seen again.

On July 10, 1918, the lookout of an American submarine spotted what looked like an abandoned enemy sub, wallowing in the ocean swells.

It was *UB-65*.

The captain of the American sub decided to shell the U-boat and send her to the bottom of the sea. But just before the American sub could fire, a violent explosion ripped the German sub apart.

As *UB-65* slipped beneath the waves, the American captain suddenly spotted a man standing at the bow with his arms folded across his chest, his head bowed.

On July 31, 1918, the German High Command sent out a brief message: "One of our submarines, *UB-65*, must be presumed lost, with thirty-four officers and men."

When the war was over, the captain of the American submarine said, "I am positive that nobody was aboard the U-boat when we spotted her. But I know that I saw someone standing on her bow with his arms folded across his chest."

Had the new crew been plagued by the ghost? Had they abandoned the ship out of fright? If so, what had become of them?

And what of the ghost of the first lieutenant? Did it remain on board *UB-65* on its final dive? Or did it leave the sinking sub at last, its ghostly duty done, its eternal rest assured?

A PICTURE
OF THE BRIDE

Everyone knows that a photograph
records the past. But can a photograph
also record the future?

For over twenty years, a framed sign had hung in the window of the Bithells' grocery store in Portsmouth, England. The sign stated the day of the week on which the store was closed. It was just an ordinary sign, with no particular importance, and none of the Bithells had paid much attention to it.

Two weeks before their son's marriage, the Bithells decided to take the sign down and change it.

They carefully pried off the front. To their surprise, they found a large photograph underneath. Then they remembered having used the stiff photo as a backing for the sign twenty years earlier.

The picture showed the then mayor of Wigan, a county borough in northwestern England, officially opening the new health center there. The smiling mayor held a small girl, about two years old, in his arms.

The Bithells stared in fascination at the man and the child in the picture.

Twenty years earlier, the people in the photograph had been complete strangers to the Bithells. But now they recognized them immediately.

The mayor was none other than the future father-in-law of their son. And the small girl he was holding in his arms was none other than the girl their son was about to wed!

The Bithells had had a photo of the bride twenty years before their son would meet and marry her.

The Bithells' daughter, Eileen, was so struck by the

strange coincidence that she wrote to a newspaper, *The Times of London*, in 1973 to tell them about it. They, in turn, published her letter in their paper.

As for Eileen's brother, the bridegroom, he kept the photo and often joked that his wife was part of the family even before he had met her.

THE FACE IN THE MILK PAIL

The bottom of a milk pail seems an
unlikely place to confront the unknown.
But that's exactly what happened to
an English farmer's wife!

E arly one chilly morning in January 1948, Margaret Leatherland left her house to milk one of the cows on her farm.

She carried a well-worn pail that had been used on the farm for more than a generation. The can was made of aluminum and kept in spotless condition.

The day had not yet fully begun, and Margaret strode across the yard to the barn in darkness. She wasn't thinking of anything in particular. Her thoughts were more or less the same as those she had every morning she did her chores.

Margaret reached the barn and was about to place the pail underneath a cow to start her milking when her eyes widened in surprise. There was a stain at the bottom of the bucket. Margaret could have sworn she had never seen it until this morning.

By now the sun had come up, so Margaret took the pail outside the barn to see better. The stain, she discovered, made an image—the image of a man's face!

Margaret was interested, but not especially frightened. Stains can sometimes look like pictures, the way this one did. The bucket probably just needed a good cleaning, she thought. She went back inside to finish her milking. Later, after she had finished her chores, she scrubbed the pail thoroughly.

Then she lifted it up to look inside. The face was still there—and it was staring back at her as if it were trying to tell her something.

Margaret was a no-nonsense type of woman. She didn't believe in ghosts or the supernatural. Although the face puzzled her, she didn't believe it was anything more than her eyes playing tricks on her. The stain was just that: a stain. She just hadn't cleaned the pail well enough, she told herself. This time she scrubbed the bottom of it until her arms ached.

But the face was still there, even clearer than before! And from its expression, Margaret couldn't get over the feeling that it was trying to give her some message.

Margaret was disturbed. Something strange *was* happening, after all. She ran to tell her husband about the mysterious face in the pail.

At first, Mr. Leatherland refused to take her story seriously. When he examined the bucket, he laughed. "The pail is just discolored," he said. "It's about time to get a new one anyway."

Meantime, he offered to clean the pail himself. He scoured it for about twenty minutes. Then he too began to feel spooked. The face in the pail had become even more distinct!

The Leatherlands could no longer treat the occurrence as a joke or a trick. Margaret began to believe that a supernatural event was taking place.

She studied the face more closely. Suddenly she gasped. "Don't you notice something about that face?" she asked her husband. "I had a feeling there was something familiar about it. It's exactly like my brother!"

Margaret's brother was a famous circus owner named Sir Robert Fossett.

When Mr. Leatherland peered at the image again, he had to admit that it *did* look a lot like Sir Robert.

News of the strange face in the pail quickly spread throughout the community. Many of Margaret's relatives came to the farm to see the strange sight. They all agreed that the image's resemblance to Margaret's brother was uncanny.

As the story of "the face in the pail" was broadcast, scores of journalists, psychic experts, and tourists came to see the face for themselves. They were all puzzled by the event. No one could offer any reasonable explanation for its appearance.

A few weeks went by. Then Margaret received some bad news. Sir Robert, her brother, was very ill.

A short time later, exactly one month—to the hour—after the face had appeared in Margaret's pail, her brother died.

Sir Robert Fossett had been a well-known figure. News of his death and the strange circumstances that had preceded it swept the country. Margaret and most of the other members of her family firmly believed that "the face in the pail" had been a supernatural warning, foretelling Sir Robert's death. After his death, photographs were taken of the image and sent to relatives.

No explanation has ever been found for the appearance of the face. But something *did* come to light months later.

After learning about the incident, one elderly member of the family revealed that the pail was the same one that Sir Robert used for washing his face every morning when he was a boy on the farm.

THE STRANGE CASE OF THOMAS MEEHAN

If you were dead, you would know it—
wouldn't you? Unless you were like
the man in this story . . .

T homas P. Meehan was a handsome young lawyer with a thriving practice. On February 1, 1963, he had just finished a case in Eureka, a city in north-western California, and prepared to return home to Concord, California. Concord was a good distance away.

Thomas left Eureka about 2 P.M. that afternoon. His associates recalled that he had complained that he thought he was coming down with the flu and was not looking forward to the long drive home.

Thomas had driven only a few hours when he called his wife and told her he was not feeling well and would be late getting home. His wife advised him to stop at a motel and continue the drive in the morning.

Thomas decided to take her advice. At 4:35 P.M., he checked into the Forty Winks Motel near a town called Garbersville. He was signed in by the owner, Chip Nunemaker. After he had gotten settled in his room, Thomas drove to Garbersville, intending to see a doctor at the local hospital. He arrived at the hospital at about 6:40 P.M.

"I feel like I'm going to die!" he told a nurse. The nurse nodded sympathetically and went to get a doctor. Ten minutes later, the nurse returned with the hospital doctor in tow. But Thomas had vanished.

At 7:00 P.M., Mr. and Mrs. Marvin Martin of Myers Flat, California, called the state police to report an accident. The Martins had been driving on Highway 101 when they had seen the taillights of a speeding car on the other side of the road disappear as the car swerved into the Eel River. The state police noted the time and rushed to the scene.

Back at the Forty Winks Motel, Chip Nunemaker glanced at the clock on the wall. It was 8 P.M. Just then, Thomas Meehan walked in the door. Chip smiled at his guest and asked if he was feeling better.

Thomas looked confused. "Do I look like I'm dead?" he asked. "I feel like I have died and the whole world died with me!"

Before Chip could reply, Thomas took his key and left without another word.

At about 9:30 P.M., Thomas called the front desk from his room and said he wanted to telephone his wife. He gave Chip the number. A few minutes later, a bellboy went to Thomas' room to inform him that the call could not be completed, because a storm had disrupted service. Thomas nodded silently, and the bellboy left.

An hour later, the police dredged up a mud-filled car from the Eel River. On examining it, they learned that it was registered to Thomas Meehan of Concord. The car had been submerged up to the taillights. No body was in it, but several scattered bloodstains marked the interior. Judging from its condition, the police guessed it had gone into the river at high speed.

By the next morning, police had tracked Thomas' whereabouts to the Forty Winks Motel. But although his clothes and suitcase were still in his room, there was no sign of Thomas himself.

Three weeks later, on February 20, Thomas Meehan's body was found in the river, sixteen miles from where his car had been found. An autopsy listed the cause of death as drowning. He had been in the water for three weeks—since February 1.

The police and everyone else who heard the news were baffled. If Thomas had not drowned when his car had first plunged into the river, then what had happened? He had been seen and spoken to at the Forty Winks Motel at two different times, 8:00 P.M. and 9:30 P.M.—the last time being two and a half hours after the accident. Surely, Thomas could not have gone back to the motel at eight o'clock, tried to make a phone call at 9:30, and then returned to the river miles away to drown! And what about his strange remark, that he felt like he had died and the whole world had died with him? If he *was* dead at the time, how could he be at the Forty Winks Motel?

To this day, no one knows the answer.

Lily didn't believe in vampires. Then she met one. . . .

Early in the morning, Nathan woke her. "Lil? I don't feel good." She put her hand on his forehead. "No fever." But he was certainly pale, she thought. As pale as . . .

"That boy who stayed over last night. His name's not really Tommy," Nathan whispered in her ear. "He talked to me after you left. His real name's funny. Ahvel."

"What?" Her sleep-fogged mind churned. Where had she heard that name? In the cemetery . . . a child's grave . . .

"He was gone when I woke up," Nathan said. "He left his clothes and Bear. But he took my pajamas. I woulda let him have Bear." Nathan rubbed his neck. "Ow. Something's bitten me."

"A mosquito, maybe."

She looked, finding two reddish punctures. Like the marks teeth might make—sharp teeth spaced about an inch apart. What would make a bite like that? Raising herself on one elbow, she gently touched the wounds, forcing her hands to stop trembling. Ahvel.

No. Not possible. Trying to swallow the tightness in her throat, she sat on the edge of the bed, remembering scary stories she'd read, of people using garlic to protect against evil beings, like werewolves. Or vampires. . . .

Ahvel . . . I pray nothing will disturb you, the old woman had said. What if the garlic she had placed on the grave was supposed to keep him there? And because Lily had taken the bulbs away, he could now get out.

No. That little boy she'd tucked in last night—he couldn't be a vampire. But suppose he were? She gazed horror-stricken at Nathan, curled up beside her. If the stories were right, if Ahvel fed on her brother until he died, then he might become a vampire, too. . . .

To find out more about Ahvel and his other undead companions, read the Trophy Chiller VAMPIRES: *A Collection of Original Stories*, **edited by Jane Yolen and Martin H. Greenberg. (This selection is from "Ahvel" by Mary K. Whittington.)**

And be sure not to miss these other books in the Trophy Chiller series:

NIGHTWAVES: *Scary Tales for After Dark* **by Collin McDonald**

THE PIT **by Ann Cheetham**